Charles Darwin

Published in the United States of America by Cherry Lake Publishing
Ann Arbor, Michigan
www.cherrylakepublishing.com

Content Adviser: Ryan Emery Hughes, Doctoral Student, School of Education, University of Michigan
Reading Adviser: Marla Conn MS, Ed., Literacy specialist, Read-Ability, Inc.
Book Design: Jennifer Wahi
Illustrator: Jeff Bane

Photo Credits: ©PD-1923 Ellen Sharples, 5; ©Matthew J Thomas/Shutterstock Photos, 7; ©PD-1923, 9;
©Milkovasa/Shutterstock, 11; ©Gregory Dean/Shutterstock, 13; ©Jess Kraft/Shutterstock, 15, 22; ©PD-1923
J. Cameron, 17, 23; ©PD-1923, 19; ©Everett Historical/Shutterstock, 21; Cover, 10, 12, 14, Jeff Bane; Various
frames throughout, ©Shutterstock Images

Library of Congress Cataloging-in-Publication Data has been filed and is available at catalog.loc.gov

Printed in the United States of America
Corporate Graphics

About the author: Czeena Devera grew up in the red-hot heat of Arizona surrounded by books. Her childhood bedroom had built-in bookshelves that were always too full. She now lives in Michigan with an even bigger library of books.

About the illustrator: Jeff Bane and his two business partners own a studio along the American River in Folsom, California, home of the 1849 Gold Rush. When Jeff's not sketching or illustrating for clients, he's either swimming or kayaking in the river to relax.

I was born in England in 1809.
I had four sisters and one brother.

My family was rich. My father was a doctor. My grandfather studied plants.

I went to college when I was 16. My father wanted me to be a doctor like him. I didn't want to be a doctor.

What do you want to be when you're older?

I liked studying nature. I gathered beetles. It was my favorite **hobby**.

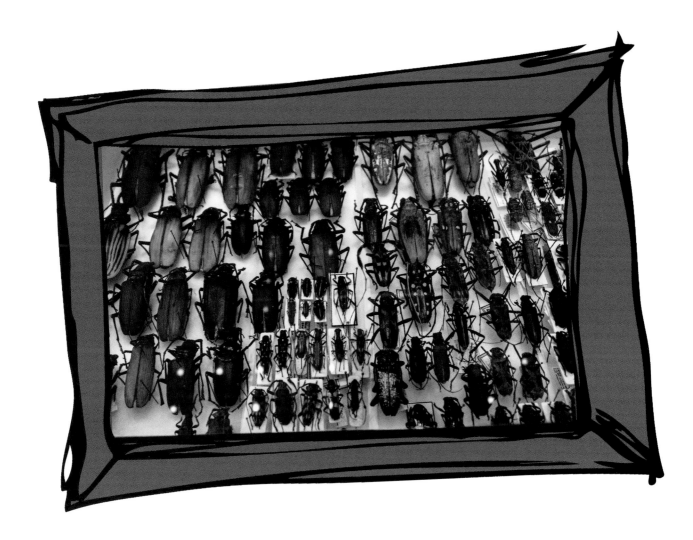

Many people were **religious** during my time. I was too. I was going to be a **priest**.

I went on a trip after college. I took many notes about what I saw and heard. I had **theories** on **evolution**.

My ideas went against my church's beliefs. I was scared to **publish** them. But my friends said I should.

When have you faced your fears?

My work made me famous. Some people agreed with my ideas. But some didn't.

What do you do when you don't agree with someone?

I died in 1882. People mostly believed my ideas by then. I changed the way people thought about **biology**. Today, I am known as the "father of evolution."

What would you like to ask me?

1831

1800

Born
1809

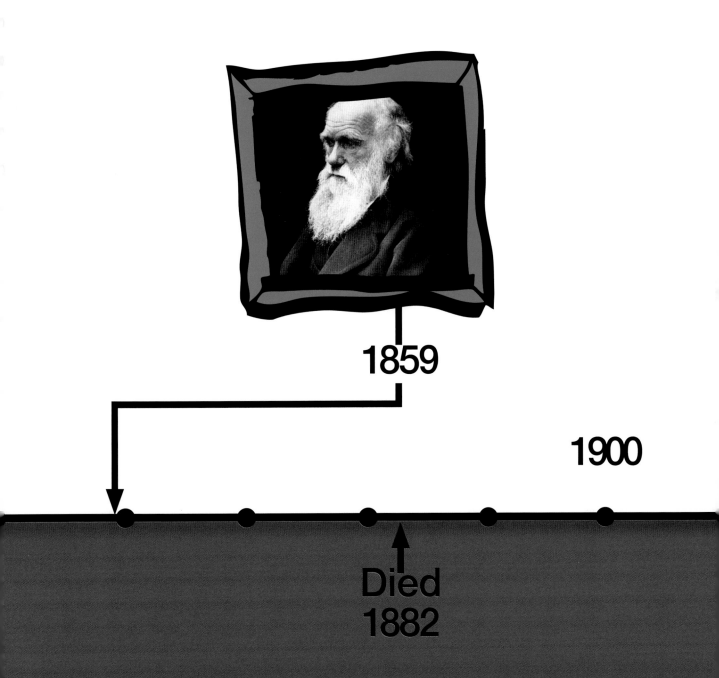

1859

1900

Died
1882

23

glossary

biology (bye-AH-luh-jee) the study of life and of all living things

evolution (ev-uh-LOO-shuhn) the slow change of living things that takes place over a long time

hobby (HAH-bee) something that you enjoy doing when you have free time

priest (PREEST) a person who leads services in certain religions

publish (PUHB-lish) to print a book, magazine, newspaper, or other material so that many people can read it

religious (rih-LIJ-uhs) describes someone who believes in a religion and follows its teachings

theories (THEER-eez) ideas or beliefs that explain how or why something happens

index